No More!

WHEN BEING A VICTIM OF SEXUAL ABUSE
IS NO LONGER AN OPTION

Lynn Meyer

Table of Contents

Acknowledgments

I want to thank my husband, siblings, family, and friends for supporting me in my healing with this book. I love you all and appreciate you so much!

Dedication

This book is dedicated to all of the surviving warriors of sexual abuse. This project was cathartic, difficult, exhilarating and scary but absolutely worth it. I realize this was not just me telling my story, but it is a healing resource to help beautiful people just like you.

Shift from the Blame by saying, "No More!"
FOREWORD BY ALISSA R.JONES

People stare when you walk by. Body language goes from relaxed to tense in a glimpse. They look and yet you can easily detect that they're trying not to see. They listen and still they don't always hear. There's something about you that makes them uncomfortable. Maybe it's the history of pain that still lingers in your eyes, maybe they can still hear your soul cry, and maybe it's the scars as they would put it, but you describe as medals. Whatever it is, it's easy for someone like you to stand out in a crowd and whatever those reasons are, the crowd has made up their mind about who you are based on their own perception of you. But there comes a time when everything changes. Where people go from staring at you to donning looks of admiration for you. Body language goes from tense to making them stick out their chest to acknowledge your bravery. They go from looking to seeing and take one step further to go from hearing to understanding. They go from being uncomfortable to resting in the peace that resides within you like a baby lying in the warmth of their mother. There comes a time when, in the eyes of others, they stop seeing you as a victim to seeing you as a Survivor; a hero if you will and the transition for both you and those who are placed in your presence, only occurs from the moment you open your mouth to share your story.

See, I share my story every chance I get. Not to be accepted by people but because, I too, was one who stared at myself when I walked past the mirror and the glimpse made me tense. I looked at me, even the assailants and tragedies, and tried my best not to see. I even asked for help and truth be told, people heard me loud and clear but still refused to listen. They turned their helping hand away because the truth left them rattled and uneasy.

Why?

Maybe they were or are still victims. Maybe, in their past, they had the opportunity to offer a helping hand of rescue and each time they saw me, I became the mirror which displayed a reflection they were ashamed of. Maybe they too didn't like their own reflection.

Rather than welcome me and love me with open arms, they rejected me. Rejection carries a sting that makes you tired of trying to explain to people why you are the way you are, why you look the way you look, and why you do the things you do. People have a tendency to make up their own minds about what they see and hear from others. After a while, you can become tired of trying to whisper through the brick walls of rejection and are eventually pushed into silence.

Rejection acts similar to an assailant and/or a tragedy and the only thing that can make you more than a conqueror and assert your authority is to open your mouth and in your full voice, and tell the unapologetic truth. That's why I refuse to be silent. It's not to make people "feel better" about me but it's about never going back to where I would once again become mastered by the bondage of silence. Not in any way, shape, or form, but by any means necessary I will never again be mastered by the bondage of silence.

Our silence is our defeat and our voice is our power. Silence is defined as the complete absence of sound and on the contrary, sound signifies that there is life left within the vessel it's coming from. When we sound off with our voice, we are simply saying to the stones that were thrown at us, we are still alive and I'm going to tear you down one by one, and build something better, something greater, out of you. We may have been broken or may even be broken, but we are mending the same way our Heavenly Father made our skin to mend when cut, which is to rush to the site of injury and minister to it with the life left in the body so that the healing process begins.

The point of a tragedy is to silence you. To leave you internally still until you die. Closing your mouth doesn't allow the soul to breathe and therefore leaving you to suffocate in misery unto death. No movement equals no strength and no strength equals no life. A life unlived and a testimony untold are simply chains unbroken and the only way to break these chains that lock up the soul and spirit is to speak the unapologetic truth. That means we take no blame in what happened. That means that we do not cover for predators of any sort. That means that we intentionally show our scars. That means that we blatantly share our story with no holds barred.

Most times, those who have a victim mentality, are looking for a way to take on some of the blame in order to avoid taking in all that really happened. When you think about what you could have done or should have done, you share in the blame as if you helped devise a plan against yourself. Would you ever sit down with the devil and help him come up with a plan for your demise? No, you wouldn't! I hear stories of survival all of the time and sometimes there are underlying ideas that the victim had a part to play in hurting themselves along with the victimizer. We have to stop associating the tragedy with our ownership for the sake of making what happened more excusable and even unreal. Even if there was something else you could have done to prevent or stop a tragedy from occurring, it does not mean that you wanted what happened to you to happen to you.

Being unapologetic is the refusal to regret, apologize, cover-up, and sugar coat what really occurred and who did it. Your family members may turn their backs on you for telling the truth. Your "friends" may walk away from you for telling the truth. None of them know exactly how you feel nor what you're experiencing as a result of the tragedy that occurred and if you decide to make them comfortable by agreeing to the placing of wool over your eyes, then you become silenced all over again.

This is why this Memoir **"No More!" "When Being a Victim of Sexual Abuse is No Longer An Option" by Lynn Meyer** is a MUST READ. Before this very moment, I remember Lynn being silenced by the very story you will read today. **"No More!" "When being a victim of sexual abuse is no longer an option"** is more than a title "It's a Movement" of every Survivor that has a story held inside of them needing someone to share their story to empower the next survivor. Let the words in the following pages inspire and motivate you to move pastALL the things that have happened to you by circumstance. Even though it happened, it not the END of your story. It is your time to rewrite the story and understand that YOUR STORY isn't for YOU, but the Survivor struggling to let go.

Although we don't understand the Whys, God chose us to go through ALL we've been through to use the very PAIN that tried to destroy us as POWER. So in closing, enjoy the POWER of Lynn Meyer's journey to Healing and Shift from the Blame that will empower you in saying "**No More!**"

From Trauma to Triumph
FOREWORD BY ADRIENNE E. BELL

When I first met Lynn, I had the pleasure of watching her fearlessly tell her story in a room full of fearless men and women who shared similar experiences. The bravery she displayed as I watched the crowd simultaneously clutch their pearls while delighting in her seamless presentation was refreshing to watch. Lynn delivered her story of childhood sexual abuse at the hands of her biological father with such power and conviction. She never spoke from a place of bitterness or blame but one of love, honor, and respect. This is NOT a self-help book motivating you to hate your abuser, rather it is a life manual teaching you the tools to overcoming traumatic circumstances against all odds. The trauma and tears this fearless storyteller endured ends in tremendous triumph!

I am so grateful for Lynn's gracious tenacity and fierce focus in helping others heal from their trauma and leading them on to triumph! Get ready to find hope, humor, and healing as you walk through the pages of this book. I promise you will NEVER be the same!

Adrienne E. Bell
Founder, The Fearless Storytellers' Movement

Everybody was thinking I was the REAL DEAL,
but I was really living a counterfeit life.

POOR BABY...

I didn't realize how lost and broken I really was until I starting writing this book. To be completely transparent, the word that describes me during the most difficult time of my life is "Counterfeit". You know how counterfeit money looks so appealing and can pass for being real? People get excited about it because they think they are handling real currency but it's FAKE! It's like if YOU put a lighter to it, it would BLAZE the hell up! LOL. The worst part is, it can be passed off to so many people because to the natural eye, you can't tell if it's counterfeit or not. Unless you are a person with a trained eye, the average consumer wouldn't really know what to look for. When you go to a bank, there is a machine that confirms whether the money is real or fake. There is also a tool called the Counterfeit Detector Pen that with one quick stroke, it confirms its authenticity. I was walking around being counterfeit, and NOBODY had that keen eye. Nobody had that pen. Nobody dared to tell me, "You are fake as hell!" Everybody was thinking I was the REAL DEAL, but I was really living a counterfeit life. Yep, I said it! Just straight up phony. I knew how to clean up a MESS, and that's exactly what I did. I think that is why God has blessed me with the spirit of counsel because I have SEEN people being disingenuous because I was one of those people...COUNTERFEIT AS HELL!!

What happens when you remain fake? You begin to become engulfed in the phoniness; it becomes your way of living. I had pretended so long that I didn't really know who I was any longer. Though I was uncomfortable living a counterfeit life, I didn't know how to get out. I felt stuck and wondered if there would ever be a way to escape. When you're hiding, you're hurting. Now, take a moment and think about ways you are hiding and why. For ladies, we wear makeup, hair, nails, and whatever else to hide behind the pain. Okay, okay, I 'm not talking about the ladies that are enhancing their beauty, but the ladies that feel they must cover up the "ugly" they don't like about themselves. For the men that may be reading this book, you cover up, too. We all have used clothes, smiles, people, and much more to cover up. What makes us do this? Are we afraid? What is the reason? Why are we hiding? I was in a state of denial. I was masking the pain, hurt, anguish, and turmoil with being counterfeit. The reason to address this counterfeit life is to begin to heal. The healing process is difficult and I believe this is the reason people avoid it. It was most certainly the reason I was doing it. You have to face what is giving you so much pain. Being vulnerable can also be another reason to not work on healing. Whatever your reason is to avoid healing, make that your reason to heal. Maybe it's shame, blame, guilt, fear of being labeled, misunderstood, fear of not being heard or believed. Whatever is the cause, use that to fuel your steps to healing. James Baldwin wrote, " Not everything that is faced can be changed, but nothing can be changed until it is faced". You can learn from adversity and vulnerability. Now, take another moment and think about a goal you've found to be quite difficult, but you managed to accomplish. You put your mind to it and made sure you didn't stop no matter how hard it was because you knew the end result was worth it. You didn't give up! You kept going and you pressed on. This is no different. Fight like your life depends on it. Fight, because you are worth it.

Let's discuss worth. In my humble opinion, self-esteem and self-worth are two different things. I see self-esteem as confidence in oneself and self-worth is the value of oneself. Looking over my life, I didn't have much of either. I made knee-jerk decisions solely based on circumstances and emotions. I was so messed up that I didn't care about the choices I made, but then as I type this, I did care. I wanted to care, I wanted to be cared for, loved, wanted, desired, and appreciated. I was pretending that I was strong and bold, but I was weak and afraid. Though I was able to come out of this being a survivor, I was a victim for so long. I accepted what society called a victim and was comfortable being in that place. Who was I to say that I wasn't a victim? Didn't I fit the criteria?

The definition of **victim** is "a person who has been attacked, injured, robbed or killed by someone else or a person who is cheated or fooled by someone else."

A victim is also someone who is harmed by an unpleasant event such as an illness or an accident.

Yep, this was me. That's who I was and there was no denying it. I started to enjoy the victim role. I was getting attention from people that felt sorry for me. My favorite was "Poor baby, I'm sorry that happened to you." I was excited and I looked forward to telling my story over and over to whoever would listen because I wanted sympathy. I was a sympathy hog and I couldn't get enough attention from people who felt sorry for me. I wondered, who else can I tell so I can get more attention? Being a victim turned me into a sick person. I wanted to receive the awkward stares, silence, and affection. I didn't care who it came from or how they gave it to me, I just wanted attention. I *needed* it. Have you ever seen a child who has fallen and looks around the room to see who noticed just to capture a sympathetic gaze from an adult and gets nothing? What happens? That child begins to wail, throw a fit, overreact and demonstrate full dramatics. That child was me. I sought after the affection of others because I desperately desired it. I was messed up, period.

Love. How I wanted it so or was it acceptance I was longing for? Is there a difference between Acceptance and Love? I thought the two were synonymous for quite some time. They are truly different. I fell into the wrong crowd for about two years trying to be accepted by a group of friends. They were the cool kids who were smart, did whatever they wanted and lived carefree. It was a strange concept to me. Wow! What is it like for NO ONE to tell you what to do? Boy, did I want that! Remember when Guess jeans were popular? Oh man, I wanted a pair. It seemed like ALL my peers had them. I *begged* my mom for the designer jeans. I was willing to settle for any piece of apparel, it didn't matter, as long as it had *Guess* on it somewhere. I got my first Guess sweatshirt one day only to find that I hadn't reached a level of utopia. I was disappointed. I was glad my mom found the sweatshirt, but it didn't complete me, fill the void, give me courage or whatever I thought it would do. I figured out then that a stupid designer shirt or item wasn't going to get me accepted into anything. Yes, obtaining this sweatshirt was going to make me more popular or change the way people saw me but the truth is, what I wanted was love. True, unconditional love. I realized at a very early age that Love is an action. It's something you DO not just say It's not a feeling, it's showing the person you love them. I noticed it wasn't just a word, but it was what was missing in my life and it took me years to finally collide with it.

There are three lessons you will learn after reading this book:

1. **Learn** that healing, restoration and transformation are possible for you. I know obtaining wholeness may seem foreign to you right now but trust me, they are attainable and waiting for you.
2. **Realize** that obtaining healing, restoration and transformation will be a tough road to travel but you will learn that perseverance and resilience are inside of you.
3. **Believe** and know that you are worth the work it will take for you to live the life in which you have always dreamed of. Let me show you how amazing and worthy you really are.

As you read through my story, do NOT feel sorry for me. I am not a victim, I am a survivor! **NO MORE** will I sit back and keep silent about my story. **NO MORE** will people be in my presence and feel as though they have no one to turn to. **NO MORE** is being a victim of sexual abuse an option. The worst time of your life is over and once you finish this book, you will realize the best is STILL to come!

*I didn't know what was really going on, but
I knew something wasn't right.*

CHAPTER 1

Just Fakin' It

I AM THE YOUNGEST of seven children in total, 4 girls and 3 boys. I grew up in Dallas, Texas and I love Mexican food, Stevie Wonder and the arts in general. I can be a bit silly, and I love my family. When I think about my upbringing, it consisted of my dad being the authoritative figure from a distance while my mom was the present peacemaker. Neither one of them was nurturing in the way I needed them to be. I think my mom was trying to keep the peace that she forgot to show affection with hugs and kisses. As small children, we didn't have a choice of whether or not we could attend church. My mom was diligent about us going to church. Even though some of us strayed away from God, I always knew I needed Him in my life.

Throughout my childhood all the way up to my teens, my family always saw me as a high achiever. Everyone expected me to have good grades because they saw me as the smart child...the intelligent child...the child who never got in trouble. I was always quiet, but very kind and well-rounded. Even though I stayed out of trouble, except during the year and a half I "acted out", I was always performing on stage. Singing, dancing, acting--you name it...that was me. But little did they know, on the inside... I was extremely shy and you really couldn't tell because I always wanted to perform. I was looked at as the person who excelled when all the while that's not who I really was. Even my teachers would say, "Oh, she's so good in class! I NEVER have a problem with her. She's one of my favorite students! She's such a bright student and a great helper." I was voted best citizen every year of my elementary years. All my teachers adored me from elementary through graduate school. I was a nerd that didn't have to study. As a child, I didn't dream of getting married, Prince Charming, or the rescuing knight. I dreamt of dying and running away, wanting to escape my parents. I remember as a very young child (between 6-8) I thought of suicide. Oh my goodness, as I write these words, I am picturing that sad little girl. She was hurting so much. I didn't realize how much I needed an outlet, and that outlet became music. I played "Someday We'll All Be Free" by Donnie Hathaway over and over almost daily. At the time I didn't know the true meaning of the song, I just know it spoke to me. This song truly saved my life. Today when I hear the song, it takes me back to a place when I was hurting, but now that I am in my healing place it's a bittersweet feeling. Music continues to be therapeutic for me.

Okay back to my parents. I hated them being together; I hated their marriage, I hated everything they stood for in my life. Individually, they behaved as if they were from two different planets. My mom was always at my recitals, games, performances, plays, concerts, and track meets. Whatever I did she was there, and I will always love her for that! My dad, on the other hand, was a lonely man who was dying inside and didn't know how to express himself properly. He was never taught love, so I felt sorry for him. My father grew up without a loving family household. It was explained to me that he didn't have a father figure. His dad left him and his brother (my uncle), to fend for themselves. The story is that they frequently ate from trash cans and were left to make decisions that the adults should have made for them had they been present. Now, again, this is the story I have been told. Sadly, I do believe it happened. The relationship my dad had with his mom was horrible. How should I describe it, "I hate that bitch!" is what my dad always said when asked about his mother. I shied away from any mention of her and prayed others would also. It was reported to me that my mother comes from a family where her mom was mean, very strict and a father that was a womanizer. I don't know too much about my maternal grandfather, but my grandmother told me he had girlfriends. My mother grew up in a house where she was taught it was okay for a man to disrespect you, hence the girlfriends he had all the while being married to my grandma.

Both of my parents had very dysfunctional childhood experiences. They were both taught unhealthy emotional habits that bled over into every relationship they ever had, especially with their children. My mother had another husband before my dad, and he beat her just like my dad did. My dad used to beat my mother for no reason. Oh wait, I have reasons: she didn't do what he said, or fast enough, long enough, correctly or just because he wanted to hit something.

All valid reasons to me... NOT! This is what he did for many years, and tried to take her life on at least one occasion. He tried to push her out in front of an 18-wheeler truck, but my sister saved her.

Do you see the dysfunction yet? Blatant disrespect from childhood had my mom thinking that it was okay for a man to treat you how he wanted and that nothing would be done about it. She wasn't taught to value or love herself. Such a damn shame.

Daddy's Little Girl

When you hear people say, *Daddy's Little Girl,* it is usually a term of endearment. The term usually describes a little girl who is adored and often spoiled by her father. The little girl is vehemently protected by her father who takes pride in guarding her very being with his own life. I wish I could say this was true for me, but it was just the total opposite. The first experience I remember was my sister washing me up in the bathroom sink. I was probably 3-5 years old, and I thought even then, "Why is she washing my butt in the sink?". I vividly remember my mom bathing me in the same manner. It happened so frequently that I thought this was the way to take a bath. At this early age, I didn't know what was really going on, but I knew something wasn't right. I also remember my dad would appear right before or immediately after I had been "washed up". It wasn't until my teenage years when I realized that my mom and sister were cleaning me to get me "ready" for my dad or he had already touched me, and they were cleaning me up. I know my sister didn't want to do this and questioned why she had to. By no means did she agree with what was happening to me; she was only a young teenager herself. She was confused and disappointed and didn't feel like she had a big enough voice to stop what was happening to her baby sister.

But you know who did have the power to stop my father from molesting me? My mother. I hated her "weakness" for allowing her husband to touch me. I was her baby, her child, her blood. How could she do this to me? I had these thoughts for many years. I resented the fact that she couldn't stand up for herself or her children. I didn't understand the concept of how a mom could not stand up for her children or protect them no matter who caused harm to them. My mom allowed the abuse to continue for years and years. This shit didn't stop until we moved out of the house. I began to block out certain days in my life. It was my body's way of protecting me. (BUT) Damn it protected me so much I don't remember half of my kindergarten up to third grade.

I never wanted to be around my dad. I didn't want to be anywhere he was. He would make me kiss him, hug him or be near him. I remembered other experiences where he would touch me and rub my butt, make me sleep next to him and would be close to me. I was so confused. Where could I run and hide? Nowhere! I was stuck. I was trapped. As time progressed, I began to act out sexually. I started masturbating somewhere around the ages of five or six, and I didn't care where I would do it. I remember being in classrooms, under my bed, and even in front of people. I didn't care when I did it. It was like my body craved the feeling. My body was so out of control; I did whatever I had to do to relieve myself. I would also act out sexually with family members and friends. This is what my dad taught me. Deep down inside I knew I was wrong, but I didn't know how to stop. I felt disgusting.

The Great Pretender

I was shy and terrified to perform even though I was great at it. I enjoyed performing and being involved in extracurricular activities. In junior high and high school, I was in track and choir. I had solos and sang in duets. I was often put out in front. When I got to college, I became captain of the cheerleading squad. Performing was something I enjoyed doing, but I always had stage fright. I would be nervous about how the performance would turn out, but it would turn out great! When I would express to people how shy I was they would say, "Girl, stop playin'. I KNOW you're not shy!" But I really was. Actually, I am still shy to a certain extent. I am an extrovert and enjoy being in the front of a room, especially when I am passionate about something. I love commanding an audience and seeing other people enjoy themselves. You could call me "The Great Pretender" because I had the ability to be stoic and act like nothing ever bothered me. I know it may sound like I am off my rocker, but I am just complex. Trauma has its way of allowing creativity to flow. In my career as a licensed therapist, it has been my experience that most people who have experienced trauma are highly creative and somewhat complex. For example, I have the tendency to be very introverted and reserved from time to time because that is how I refuel myself.

On the other hand, I have extrovert qualities because I love being around people and entertaining. Who taught me to be a performer? Who taught me to be "The Great Pretender"? My parents because they taught me how to lie. They taught me how to adjust and become whatever they expected me to be. I am not saying this to blame them, but I want you to understand that is how I became so great at performing. I am saying this to share my truth that when you live a lie for so long that even YOU begin to believe it, that's when you have to say to yourself, "NO MORE!" Don't be discouraged if it seems as if you are all over the place or like you have multiple personalities. Embrace who you are and make the adjustments needed to be your true, genuine self, even when no one is looking!

Acting Out...

I was a good kid growing up, but I think I was about 15 or 16 years old when my life began to change for the worse. I met this girl who I thought was quite intriguing. I was a sophomore in high school, and she was a senior. I began acting out the moment I started hanging out and rebelling with her. She was a very bad influence on me, but I didn't know that at the time because in school she seemed to be really smart. We had choir together so you would always find us harmonizing and just having fun. Our peers always wanted us in their group because we sang well together. She had a beautiful alto voice, and I was a strong first soprano. As time progressed, we were virtually inseparable. One day, we were hanging out after school, and I shared a secret with her. I had a crush on one of her guy friends since the beginning of the school year, so I finally told her. She said, "Oh, yeah. He's a really good guy, and you should try to talk to him!" Remember back in the day when you would write a letter to your crush and it would say, "Do you like me? Check *Yes, No,* or *Maybe*? Well, I did NOT do that. Instead, I decided to write my crush this long letter expressing to him how much I liked him and wanted to be with him. Why did I do that?! He was really good in English so instead of being flattered that he received the letter, he spent more time tearing my letter apart! His response was, "Your punctuation isn't right!" I was so embarrassed at how he rejected and humiliated me when I had nothing but good intentions. I just wanted him to know I liked him! Who cares about the punctuation? When I think back, I never should have written that letter because it was evidence of how desperate I was for attention from this guy...but I digress. My friend was so supportive and said, "Hey, don't worry about that. It's okay. You're still a catch. Just ignore him." A few days later as we were just hanging out like we normally did when she blurted to me and said, "I like you!" In my innocence, I was like, "Oh, I like you, too. You are really cool!" She said, "No, I *REALLY* like you." At first, I sat there thinking, "Didn't we already talk about this? But then it dawned on me that she was into me like I was into her guy friend. Me? With a girl? I never had a same-sex attraction before, so this seemed to be coming out of nowhere. I liked her as a person because she was extremely intelligent, but as time progressed, she had a dark side that intrigued me even more. As time went on, we became closer and closer. The thing that brought us even closer was when her mother became very sick and eventually passed away. I felt so sad for her that she had lost her mom and I did my very best to be there for her. Even my family was supportive of her and felt just as bad that she had lost her mom. We would always spend the night at each other's house. My mom cared for her just as if she was one of her own children. Even some of my siblings thought she was pretty cool. My dad pretty much stayed to himself, so I don't really know what he thought about her, but for the most part, my family fully embraced her. One day we were hanging out at her house and all of a sudden, she kissed me. I was stunned because she knew I liked boys so I was wondering, "Should I kiss her back?" I still didn't like her like that, but I was attracted to the fact that this is something my parents would **not** approve of. We started hanging out even more so much to the point where I would miss curfew. I was excited that this was something I could do to rebel against my parents. Once I started breaking the rules, that's when my parents said to me, "STOP hanging with her. She is a bad influence on you!" I had no intention of stopping and I knew full well that my parents did not approve of my friendship with her, but frankly, I didn't care. I was so tired of trying to be the child THEY wanted me to be versus the person I wanted to be. I was thinking to myself, "You guys didn't protect me so NO, I'm not gonna follow the rules!" The more I knew my parents hated me being with her, the closer we became. Eventually, I started drinking (which I hated and got sick every time) and engaging in sexual encounters with this girl. In my mind, I still knew that I didn't like her like that, I just liked the fact that I was rebelling against my parents. That's what brought me the greatest pleasure. She sold marijuana and got into all sorts of trouble. Not only did her mom pass away but her father was nowhere to be found. All she had was her older sister, so she really wasn't being raised by anyone at all. This fit right into my design of rebellion. I was spinning out of control, and I didn't care. I would engage in risky behavior like sneak out of the house at night and even skip school. I would tell my parents I was with someone else when I was actually with her. I had missed so much school that I was in danger of being held back. By this time, my "friend" had already graduated from high school and was in college at this point. I was only a junior in high school, and I was about to throw my life away. My mom stepped in and got a doctor's note to cover the days I had missed just so I wouldn't be held back.

So for about a year, between ages of 15-16 ½ I was a terror! I acted out to the point where I would run away from home to meet this girl and have sex with her. When I say, "acting out" I really mean, "crying for help." I began doing reckless things just to numb the pain and anger I felt towards my family. I would do impulsive things like speed race at dangerously high speeds. My reckless and impulsive behavior could have landed me in jail because I could have hurt someone or even myself! I could have killed someone or myself, but I just didn't care. I never wanted to be with her it was just the thrill of being disobedient. That's what I was in love with...rebellion. I was using this girl for rebellion just as much as she was using me for entertainment. I would lie to my parents and tell them I was going to a party, but actually, I was meeting up with my "girlfriend." My mom was so frustrated with me to the point where I literally saw her aging. Over the course of one year, she started looking older because my acting out was taken a toll on her body. But I still did not care. I did not care because I was so hurt and I wanted both of my parents to hurt too! It is true what they say, "Hurt people hurt people."

I don't want to hurt anyone; I just want to tell the truth.

CHAPTER 2

Tell The Truth and Stop The B.S.

I DON'T WANT TO hurt anyone; I just want to tell the truth. I had no idea that I would be a victim who would turn into a survivor. As I stated before, my dad physically abused my mom, siblings and me. I mentioned the abuse that was given to my mom, but I only touched the surface on what I am aware of and what I witnessed concerning my siblings. Part of my healing is sharing these experiences with you. For years, I struggled with sharing or keeping quiet. I didn't want to hurt anyone in my family. I thought if I told anyone that my family would be dysfunctional, but we were already, so I really had nothing to lose.

I remember watching my dad put a gun to my brother's head because he didn't water the grass. The entire house was in an uproar. Everyone was a total wreck...crying, screaming, begging and pleading for my dad to put the gun down. It was a madhouse. Can you believe it? All because my brother didn't water the freaking grass. During those years, my dad was an idiot and never learned how to talk to his kids. Beatings, belittling, and scare tactics were his weapons of choice when he called it "disciplining" us. One of my sisters told me of a time when my dad beat her like she was a man because of a choice she made. She said he beat me like I was a stranger, and that he never apologized for it. She stated that she knew she needed to get out of the house. There was another incident I learned about when my oldest brother had enough of my dad beating up on my mom. Finally, he told my dad, "If you touch my mama again, I'm going to kill you." My dad didn't like being challenged, but he was a coward, so he backed off. He knew my brother was serious. That's the day he started to hate my brother.

Ruined relationships are what my dad experienced his entire life. I don't remember a time my dad sat us down to talk about a situation or problem. He never fathered us or gave us loving instruction. Everything he did was based on intimidation and fear. In my heart, I believe he was tormented by fear as well because he had no idea how to be a father. Regardless of that, he was DEAD WRONG on so many levels and was never challenged by my mom. We were so afraid of him that **no one** ever challenged him until we got older. Fear was the doorway to anxiety, depression, alcoholism, mental and physical challenges that plague my family to this day.

Not only was my dad abusive, but he was an adulterer. He had affairs with so many different women. His selfish desires were the only thing that mattered. I would intercept calls when the girlfriend would call. She would do the "call once and hang up" crap and I hated it! I was very smart for my age, and I caught on to that fast. One day I got the call instead of my dad, and this heifer had the nerve to pretend she had the wrong number. I said to her, "You know you don't have the wrong number. You know exactly who you called. Don't call this house anymore, disrespecting my mother again". I don't remember any more of those calls unless they changed up the way they communicated. I also remember another occasion where my dad was selfish. He invited the mistress to my sister's wedding. I can recall him trying to introduce me to a lady and a child that looked like me. He was so nonchalant about the introduction saying, "This is Princess." My dad had called me Princess my entire life, and now he was trying to introduce me to his other family. I gave all of them a dismissive and disgusting look and walked away. I wasn't stupid. He didn't have to tell me who the lady or her daughter was; I already knew the truth. I didn't tell my sister until after the wedding was over. She said she knew something was going on but couldn't figure it out at the time. I really didn't want to hurt her, but she needed to be told. I refused to hold on to another secret! I hate secrets! NO MORE!

"You Know How She Is"

Who am I to my siblings? Well, I'm sure they'll say that I was spoiled and got away with things and didn't have to go through much. I would have to agree, but not because I craved to be in this role. This is where my dad placed me, and for that, I was not always liked by my siblings. I remember a time when I heard my older brother say, "I don't like her." He was speaking to my mom. I heard the hurt in her voice, and all she could say was, "Why would you say that"? To my surprise, his answer was "I just don't." Unbeknownst to them I heard the whole thing and retreated to my room. I felt so bad and couldn't understand why he said such a nasty thing about his sister. I pondered on that for quite some time, but couldn't come up with an answer that was sufficient. I later concluded that it was because he saw me as my dad's favorite. I didn't understand the pain and suffering he and my other siblings shared. I was oblivious to the struggles and sorrow, and he hated me for that. Fast forward to now - we have a good relationship...that's my big bro.

I had strained relationships with my sisters too, but I think it was because of the age difference. My now oldest sister, Sandra, told me recently that she feels like we just became sisters over the past couple of years. She mentioned it was because she was leaving the house and getting married when I was younger, so the bond wasn't there. It hurt for her to say that to me, but those are her feelings, and I understand. I looked up to my sister Sina a lot and felt close to her, but I never knew if she loved me the way I loved her. She would spend time with me, having fun and being silly, but I still didn't know to what extent she cared. The brother that is closest to me in age (Kevin) was my best friend growing up. The sad thing is I never told him, but I felt my actions showed him. He was my hero in so many different situations. I remember two situations like they were yesterday.

One was a time that a custodian at my school was rushing us out, and I was drinking from the water fountain. I was trying to be obedient, so I quickly finished my drink and raised up to only hit my head on the wall. A large knot began to form quickly, and my brother was instantly angry. He was mad at that custodian, he said a few words and gave her nasty looks. I laugh when I think about this now. The second incident is when my second oldest brother (Man) tried to make me eat pig's feet. I cried and cried, but my brother Kevin said, "Don't worry, I'll eat it for you." I knew then that he had my back and I fell in love with my brother that day. I knew I had a friend in him and that he would always protect me. That was the only time a male in my life had protected me, honored me, and respected me.

I have two other siblings I haven't mentioned, the oldest brother and the oldest sister. My oldest brother (Joe) is old enough to be my father, and although we are from different generations, he loves his baby sister. We don't share the same childhood experiences, but we can converse on a level that others don't. I think it's a Virgo thing.

Well, I've saved my oldest sister, Jonice, for last. She was my best friend. We shared so many things in common from 80s music to inside jokes to our quick wit and sarcasm. Most of all we just understood one another, she got me, and I got her. She too was old enough to be my parent, but our bond was very tight. The sad part is I didn't even know she was my sister until I was about nine years old. She lived in Maryland and was sent away when she was a teenager. They said it was because she got pregnant, but I have my thoughts on that story. I truly believe my dad tried to mess with her, too. There, I said it! I think she was sent away because my father couldn't keep his hands to himself. I learned of my sister one year around Christmas time. She came to the house and I thought she was so pretty and nice, but I also thought she was my sister's friend. I had no idea this was MY sister as well. What a shame! Lies, half-truths and keeping secrets are deadly to every relationship. I felt it necessary to share a little about the relationships I have with my siblings so you can better understand me. These relationships also played a part in shaping me from childhood to my adult years.

Let me clarify something. My siblings are not aloof, neglectful or self-absorbed by any means, but growing up in a family like mine can make you think you need to stay invisible so that you didn't catch the wrath of my father. I have great relationships with my sisters and good relationships with my brothers. We all love hard and sometimes too hard. I think it's because we didn't get the love we desired or deserved. Sometimes, we give things instead of our time. NO fault to us, but this is what we were taught. My belief is we are trying to fill the void that we didn't get when we were kids. This is just speculation, but I know I'm right. (LOL). I do LOVE my siblings, and we are a dysfunctional bunch, but we are a strong unit. My second to the oldest brother said it best, "With sibling love, there are no weak links." I will always remember this piece of wisdom.

I remember another time when I was arguing with my brother Kevin. I can't remember exactly what we were arguing about but I remember him saying I was gay. I got so mad at him so I called him gay because he was wearing his hair like Prince and the argument blew up from there. At first, I was speaking to him very calmly, and then I began cursing him out. I became verbally aggressive and abusive because I was tired of him provoking me. When we got back home, we had a physical altercation in my room. I violently pushed him against my mirror causing him to break it. In walks my parents saying in unison, "Hey, what's going on here?!" Immediately, my brother started acting like he was the victim and shouted, "She started the whole thing!" and all this other crap he said I did. Funny how he never told them what HE did to provoke me. But I digress. My mother responded by saying, "Well, you know how she is." The moment those words left her lips, I was disappointed because my mom had let me down again. She didn't bother to ask what happened to me. She didn't protect me at that moment when she had the power to do so. I was even angrier because my father didn't say a word...he just stood there. I was furious because I was positive that he felt the same way my mom felt. He never said a word, but the expression on his face spoke a thousand words! In my mind, I was thinking, "YES, you DO know how I am, but I am that way because of YOU and your husband! YES, you DO 'know how she is' because of what happened to her! You didn't protect 'her' so 'she' has a valid reason to be angry! YES, you know how she is because you know the hurt behind the actions she displays." Why didn't she tell my brother the WHOLE story? "YES, we know how she is because we made her that way".

Searching For Love

Looking back now, I know that everyone I ever encountered could sense the desperation pouring out of me. I ended up in terrible relationships of all kinds. Every relationship I had whether it was a platonic friendship, intimate, business or professional, I was toxic and utterly dysfunctional. I craved attention so much that I would throw myself at anyone who would hear or see me. This destructive behavior turned into a horrible 16 years of my life repeatedly making the same mistakes. I didn't love myself!!!!!! Because I didn't love myself, I succumbed to the generational curse of dysfunctional relationships that were passed on to me by my parents. When I would get involved in new "relationships," they were always a repeat of the previous one. For instance, I would get involved with men who didn't care about me. Most of them baited me by pretending to care about me, so I thought that was an excuse to give my body to them. I was extremely promiscuous in search of true love I slept with anyone who said hello with a smile. I allowed low lives to monopolize my time and consume my very being. I didn't care what they did to me; I just wanted to be in their presence because to me it was some form of affection. I became very aggressive with my voice and actions. I found myself yelling and screaming uncontrollably nearly on a daily basis. My actions were so impulsive, and I was completely out of control. I first had sex at the age of 15, not because I was pressured but just to do the act. I thought this was what the guy wanted and I didn't think about the consequences. I just figured this was how my life would be, give it up and turn it loose. When I went away for college, I slept around with guys and messed around with girls, but again I was trying to find love. I placed myself in some very risky and dangerous situations. I was drinking like a fish, and I tried marijuana (but I didn't like it). I wanted to find something or someone that would make me forget my past. I pretended that my past didn't affect me, but it did in a tremendous way. Those around me thought I was smart, funny, confident, strong and the list goes on. The sad part was all of those were true; I just didn't believe it at the time. All I knew was that I was hurting, and I wanted to numb the pain by any means necessary. What I ended up doing was opening the wound more and pouring alcohol in it and then wondering why I was in so much pain. I am not proud of this behavior nor am I ashamed. I was a product of my environment, and this is what I was taught. This is all I knew.

I excelled in everything I did because I was trying to escape my reality. I wanted to be noticed and adored. I also wanted to be loved by my parents, siblings, teachers and everyone in my life. I found myself being a people pleaser and making poor choices with the wrong kind of people throughout my life. As I reflect on that time in my life, I feel as though most people thought I could do no wrong. I was always so polite and pleasant to other people, but I tended to be a bit flippant with my dad. I didn't realize until I started writing this book how I was kind to everyone except for my dad. Even when my mom would say things I didn't like, she never received the attitude I gave my dad. In my mind, he deserved it. I didn't realize I was wearing a mask even at a young age. No one knew the pain, terror, and torture I had been through with my father because I learned to wear the mask and wore it well. Even though I could have won an Academy Award for my "performance", I was still furious and emotionally wounded.

What was wrong with me? Why was I self-destructing? How could so much pain make me want to destroy my life? I was scared for my life, but I didn't know how to stop. I was crying out for help, but no one knew because I wore proudly wore a mask that I refused to take off. Aren't your parents supposed to protect you? At least that's what I thought. Just look at television: *The Brady Bunch, Leave it to Beaver,* and *The Cosby Show* were my "go to" for my "Perfect Family" fantasies. Oh, how I wished my life was like the kids on television, but then again I despised television for that very reason. It wasn't **my** life and I was angry. Why couldn't I have a father who loved my mom, made her smile, brought her flowers and respected her? Why couldn't I have a mom who spoke her mind? Why didn't my mother understand the value of her words, feelings, and emotions like the moms on television? Why couldn't my family be like the families are saw on television? I wanted a family who cared for each other unconditionally. Instead, I had a father from the pits of hell and a mother who was deathly afraid of him. Why couldn't I have siblings who enjoyed life? Instead, they were so messed up; they couldn't do anything but try to keep themselves alive and sane. My whole life sucked, and I didn't see a way out of this mess!

...dying to my old self was the only way to embrace my healed self.

CHAPTER 3

Dying to Self

HAVE YOU EVER started to clean your house when you realized you just didn't want to do it? You know, when you stand in your living room ready to vacuum and you think, "Maybe it can wait another day" or "Will anyone notice if I don't vacuum today?" I love a clean house, but I do not like to clean. Some people love to clean because it is a form of relaxation for them, but that's not me! I can put on some music and push through it because I love the finished product, but I do not like cleaning. After I put on my music, I say, "Okay, where am I going to start? The bathroom? The kitchen? Do I want to make the bed or start with the laundry?" As I was preparing to clean my home one day, I had this epiphany. That's how I treated my life for so long.

Did anyone know I was as dirty on the inside as I was? Was my pain seeping through my pores where others could smell it? I knew things were dirty in my life, but I wasn't sure if anyone else noticed. I asked myself, "I wonder does anyone know that I am filthy? Does anyone notice how out of order my life is?" I mastered the art of being counterfeit for so long portraying to have everything so together. I looked the part, but I was dying a slow death. I put the music on in my life to try to drown out the pain that I felt inside. I faked having fun even though I was dying daily.

I approached my need to clean up my life the same way I approached cleaning my home. I knew I needed healing, but I was NOT looking forward to going through the process of healing. Yes, I wanted to experience the finished product, but I didn't feel like smelling the stench of the past again. I didn't like the dust-like residue of anger that kept coming up in my interactions with others. I had to deal with my own "dirty laundry" once and for all. I had swept so many things under the rug for many years, and I was afraid to address the pain. I had so much chaos and counterfeit behavior going on, so I needed to decide what I was going to address first. What level of my pain was I going to confront? I knew I need to DIE to my old self and clean up my life. I knew that dying to my old self was the only way to embrace my *healed* self. This time it wasn't about ending my life, but healing it. I didn't want to die; I wanted to live.

I had to take a step back and acknowledge that I had repeatedly been molested by my father. I had to recognize the fact that I was hurt and damaged by the pain he caused. One day I was meeting with one of my clients for a regular therapy session. I had a moment of self-disclosure, and I told him it took me about 25 years to honestly admit that I was hurting. No matter how strong I seemed, I was still afraid to admit my truth. He looked at me and said, "Wow, even you?" I said, "Yes, even me." I shared that with him because I wanted him to know healing from broken places was possible.

During my personal therapy sessions, I found humor during my healing process. Nothing that happened to me was funny, but sometimes I would find myself laughing uncontrollably. When I reflected on how distorted my thoughts and feelings were, all I could do was laugh at myself. When I'd think back to how messed up in the mind I was, I found great pleasure in taking note of the dysfunction and actually having the tools to do something about it. MAN! I was sadistic and cynical. In my mind, I was a good person even though I did not feel like one. I was very clear that my thoughts were wrong, but there was a time I did not have the tools to change them. Once I submitted to therapy, it truly saved my life.

It took a LONG time for me to die to myself. I did NOT want to do it. I felt like life was easier if I remained phony. I felt protected by keeping a smile on my face and acting like everything was well. I felt like if I finally expressed my feelings, I would be ugly to myself and other people. I felt like people would be shocked at what I really looked like once I removed the mask of hurt, pain, shame, and betrayal. I thought people would say, "Oh, no! Put the phoniness back on!" I had chains on my voice, mind, heart, and soul that I always thought would have me bound forever.

Finding my voice was difficult in the beginning because I allowed it to be silenced for so many years. I knew to speak again I would need a strategy, so I began speaking life into myself daily. I spoke positive affirmations regarding my future and engaged in constant prayer along with consistent meditation every day. I started to feel alive for the first time! I wanted to feel the sun on my face. I traveled the world visiting a new place as often as I could - the Bahamas, Jamaica, Puerto Rico, Dominican Republic, and New York City to name a few. I began to enjoy my life and the amazing experiences I was intentional about creating. I no longer took my life for granted, but instead, I started to savor every waking moment.

When I began to clean my own house, I decided to start with the bathroom. I cleaned the mirror first then the sink and countertop. I knew I was going to save the disgusting toilet for last. My excitement grew because I started smelling the freshness and seeing my image in the mirror a little clearer. Then, I moved to the bathtub and the shower. The entire bathroom seemed a little brighter just because I took the time to give it some attention.

I used this same process when it came to cleaning up my life. I didn't really want to complete the cleaning process, but I did. When I started noticing myself becoming healthier, I shared my story with others. Whenever I finish cleaning my natural home, I feel amazing. It's the same feeling I experienced when I finally received my healing. I released all the negativity and anger. Almost immediately, I started feeling so much better. And you can feel better, too.

You don't have to continue to pretend. You have to be okay with the fact that you were dirty and now you are cleaning up your life. Be okay with that. You can go ahead and die to your old self. It's okay for the old you to pass away and not be with you anymore. It's okay to let the old you die so the new you can live.

"I'm done with you."

CHAPTER 4

May 22, 2002

It was May 22, 2002. I was in my third-floor apartment sitting on my purple chaise lounge where the blinds were open, and the sun was shining through. I remember this moment quite vividly because I was extremely comfortable in my clothes, but not in my spirit. I had on some boy shorts and an old theater t-shirt. Even though I was fully clothed, my spirit felt naked. I felt exposed and extremely empty. I remember thinking to myself, "What am I doing wrong? My life is not where it needs to be or should be or could be." At that moment, I was experiencing so much pain and turmoil in my body not knowing what to do or how to move forward. I felt lost and hopeless.

I just sat there with the television was playing in the background. I can't quite remember what was on, but I do remember the background noise and blurry images flashing across the screen as I sat in deep thought. I thought deeply about my life, what I had accomplished and what I still wanted to achieve. I remember my apartment being spotless. It smelled clean, but it felt dirty. Instantly, I realized that it was my mind and my soul that was feeling like that. As I sat there, I thought. "Something's really got to change." To be honest, I wasn't sure if I wanted it to change, but I knew it needed to change.

Suddenly this feeling came over me that made me feel like something was about to happen. I felt like a presence had stepped into the room preparing to address me. I wasn't sure if it was a really strong thought or if a literal presence was entering my space, but I knew SOMETHING was getting ready to happen. You know how you go to the movies and it gets dark right before the opening scene? That's what happened to me at that moment. Immediately, the scene begins with sounds of intense anguish, turmoil, and pain. The sounds of sorrow that filled the room still haunt me to this day. I didn't see actual people, but I saw black figures in this scene. The vision was so intense and extreme. My senses were in overdrive. I could hear the cries and the screams of the figures. At first, I didn't think I was actually seeing this, but it was true. I could smell and even taste the pain that I was beholding. I could literally feel the pain all through my body. All of a sudden, it seemed as if I was being lifted off the chaise. Now, my body was not elevated off the chair, but it seemed like my spirit was leaving my body and being placed inside this open vision I was having. I call it an "open" vision because I was wide awake and my senses were working at full capacity. I seemed to be suspended between two gigantic hands that cupped my body while in mid-air. Out of nowhere, I heard the words, **"I'm done with you"** and immediately my spirit began to drop into this pit. This dark hole of anguish, sorrow, and pain--my spirit was being dropped. I could feel my very soul being pulled from my body into this abyss of pain, sorrow, and sheer anguish.

At that moment, I knew that was the Lord telling me that He was tired of trying to get through to me. I heard in my spirit, "I've asked your mom, your grandma, and even your sisters to talk to you. You know what My Word says but you still choose to disobey me. Since you are not listening, this is the way I have to show you that I am serious. If you continue to go down this path, I am done with you!" I was extremely promiscuous and alcohol was my drug of choice. I was so unpredictable and my family had no idea what I would do next. Everything I did was so random. I had no rhyme or reason to the madness. I stayed out late and went to all sorts of nightclubs where I had no business being. My main goal was to piss my parents off as much and as often as possible. And it worked. All of this was going through my head at that moment, and I knew it was God talking to me. I began to violently shake and scream, "Lord, PLEASE don't give up on me!" I had never sobbed and cried so hard in my life. I was terrified because it seemed as if my life was about to end. I cried, "Lord, please give me another chance to get it right! I am so sorry! PLEASE don't give up on me!"

As I repeatedly cried out to God, the pain I felt continued. It seemed as if my very soul was on fire. I just kept saying, "Jesus, please don't turn your back on me. Please don't give up on me!" Just as suddenly as the vision occurred, that's how quickly it faded away. I continued to cry, but this time it was tears of joy because I had just been given another chance. I was given my LIFE back and an opportunity to get it right. Once I finally stopped sobbing uncontrollably, I continued to sit there in a daze thinking, "Jesus really loves me." I felt like one of God's most disobedient children because I had done so much bad in my life. In spite of all of the dirt I have done, He spared my life.

As the moments went by, I started feeling a little better. I didn't feel great, but I knew I no longer felt those feelings of torment, sorrow, and hopelessness. I was still sobbing but not as violently. I felt like a little kid whose feelings were hurt until all I could do was "the hiccup" kind of cry between breaths as the tears continued to flow. My tears turned from sorrow to gratefulness because God loved me enough to have such a divine encounter with me. He revealed His love for me in such a haunting but AMAZING way. Finally, I started feeling like a new breath of life came into my body. I got up from the chaise and began to walk around and catch my breath after what had just occurred. What seemed like hours trapped in this vision was literally only about 3-5 minutes. As I walked around the house, I began to hum, "Amazing Grace" because only God's grace could make my life brand new like He just did.

I remember saying to myself, "Look at God. Look at how He has blessed you, girl! Look at all the stuff you have done, and He STILL loves you!" I just kept going from room to room in my apartment testifying of God's grace and mercy. Remember when I said the blinds were open in the beginning? It seemed like the light shining through my window kept getting brighter and brighter by the moment. I walked over to the window and let the sun shine on my face. I was being replenished and restored at that very moment. Words cannot describe the amount of gratefulness and joy that began flooding my soul at that very moment. I felt so good, and the tears of joy just kept flowing. I just kept saying, "Thank you, Jesus. Thank you, Jesus." repeatedly as I continued to walk from room to room.

For the first time, it felt like I could breathe. For the first time, it seemed like I could see so clearly. Just a few moments prior, I thought my life was ending, but now it seemed as if I had another opportunity to begin again. I knew I had no more chances to live destructively based on the past pain I had experienced. It was time for me to live a new life as Christ as the center of it.

At that point, I walked over to the calendar and noticed the date. It was Wednesday, May 22, 2002, the day that changed my life--forever. Before that day, I was merely existing. I was going through the motions. I felt like I was programmed to do what I was told, like a robot. But again, God rescued not only my soul but my entire existence. I began to look at life with new eyes. I was never mad at God, but I did think He'd forgotten about me. After this encounter, I never had that thought again. I was finally loving on me, building my self-esteem, understanding my self-worth, and valuing my abilities and characteristics. I was a new person.

I noticed I wasn't as aggressive, mean or short with people. I wasn't as bossy or controlling. (Now, if you ask my husband he may say otherwise...LOL!) I learned how to have conversations without flying off the handle, yelling, screaming, berating others, jumping to conclusions and thinking the worst. I was finding myself, and I liked it. I began noticing what I liked and disliked from food to events and people, without feeling like I had to please others. I'm able to look in the mirror and see me, inside and out. I saw the hurt little girl who had no hope. I saw the teenager who was depressed. I saw the young lady who gave herself away because she was empty. I even noticed the adult who was confused and stagnant. I saw her. *I saw her! I saw ME!*

Beholding my full, complete and authentic self in the mirror at every stage no longer made me sad. I accepted her, at every level...flaws and all. I began to heal her by showing her compassion. I talked to her with love and kindness, but most of all I listened to her. That's right I began talking and boy, did I have a lot to say! It was like I was held captive for so long and finally, I was set free.

I had no intention of trusting him.

CHAPTER 5

Let's Be Exclusive

I MET A MAN that I didn't think was for me at a time when I was content and loving life. I was traveling and doing ME to the fullest. I was confident and carefree. I was abstinent for 12 years before meeting my husband. I felt renewed and refreshed because I felt I was detoxed from so many violations from the past. I felt like a born again virgin so even though I was not a virgin, I felt whole and complete within myself. My mind was clear of toxic emotional clutter. At least, I thought it was.

Even though I was enjoying life, I was still in a great deal of pain. It seemed he appeared almost out of nowhere. We met online and had our first date at Don Pablo's Mexican Restaurant.

He had on jeans with black and white sneakers along with a TCU polo shirt. I remember him holding two dozen yellow roses in his hand. I thought this was so sweet because NO other man had ever done this for me. "Hmm, he must be different" is what I said to myself, and he was and still is (smiling really hard right now). He was a gentleman, opening the door, allowing me to walk in front of him, choosing where to sit, letting me order first. All of this may seem small, but this was what I wanted from a man and never received. We had great conversations about life, past experiences, and the future. During the meal, he asked if he could kiss me, and I said yes. I don't kiss on the first date, but he was different and somehow I already knew he was. We were enjoying the meal and out of nowhere he said, "I want to be exclusive."

HUH?

I looked at him as if he just cursed me out or called me out of my name. "No, I don't want to be exclusive. That's not what I want." He looked at me with some disappointment and said, "Okay". Now, I didn't know that the "okay" meant game on. Before the date ended, he called his mom and said to her "I met the woman I'm going to marry." I was flabbergasted and wanted to run. This man had to be crazy, he just met me! I didn't run, I stayed and we proceeded to talk for hours. He was so laid-back and fun. He was me! We continued to date, he courted me, he was interested in me, he wanted and desired ME. I knew then I was falling in love with him.

He taught me the true meaning of love. He accepted me for who I truly was, the hurt little girl with the tumultuous past. He allowed me to expose the scars that I covered up. He has acknowledged my pain, but he never made excuses for it. One day, I was being a complete jerk, being snippy and just plain rude. There were times I remember thinking to myself, *He is just like everybody else. He is going to hurt me just like my dad and all the other men from my past.* I only felt that way because he would not allow me to have my way. There were times I wanted to properly express myself with words, but the wounded little girl inside me would speak louder than the woman. Throwing adult tantrums was normal for me. I'd slam doors, give the silent treatment, cut my eyes and just be plain mean! That day was one of those days. After a few minutes of my adult temper tantrum, he calmly said to me, "You're acting out".

With that small statement, he helped me realize that I was on the path of healing but I wasn't entirely whole. I realized that I was protecting myself from him because I saw the past guys, including my father, in him. I didn't want to be hurt again. I returned to therapy and worked out my feelings once again. I could let all the pain, resentment, sadness, depression, anxiety and whatever else I was holding on to go. Because of this, it allowed me to have a beautiful relationship with this man. It turned into a much-needed friendship filled with trust, under-standing, love, and respect. He is my best friend to this day, and most importantly, my husband.

Many individuals who have been sexually abused or violated in some way often have trouble engaging in good sexual encounters with long-term partners. Especially in marriage, reports show that women have a tough time being sexu-ally open with their husbands than others who have not. Some women feel they don't want to be touched a certain way, so their partner often has to adjust or be flexible to their mood swings when it comes to sex. I totally understand what it is like to not want to be mishandled. Some women have even reported that they hate foreplay and would rather get right to intercourse because foreplay feels too much like being molested. Even when it comes to cuddling, holding hands or any other form of non-sexual intimacy, for some people, this is off limits. That is not quite how it is with me.

When I met my husband, I never had any sexual inhibitions with him. Before meeting him, I was very promiscuous, so I was very in tune with my body. I knew what I liked and what I didn't like. My limitations were more emotional or what some would call "playful intimacy" that I didn't like. I never had issues with holding hands, hugging or anything like that. I actually love PDA (public displays of affection) but when it comes to "play intimacy" or "play wrestling" that is an absolute violation for me. For example, my brothers and nephews would also want to wrestle and play really rough, and I just didn't like that so I would become extremely aggressive. They would have to say, "Whoa, hang on! Calm down...we are just playing!" In the beginning of my marriage, my husband used to like to "play wrestle" as well, and I just didn't want that feeling of being out of control. I didn't want anyone pinning me down or making me feel like I was being restrained. When it seemed like I was being restrained, it took me back to moments where my dad would molest me, and it made me uncomfortable. The crazy part was, I never remember my dad holding me down or being aggressive with me, so I am not sure where my violent reaction came from, even to this day.

When I first met my husband, I was extremely open with him sexually. I never felt like I didn't want to be sexual with him. I have always been very affectionate and love to be around him. To this day I do not like to be completely nude around him (or anyone else for that matter), but for the most part, I am open. Some people may be just the opposite, but I just wanted to share where I am. I don't have to be all up under him, either. If he is sitting on one end of the couch and I am on another end, that's perfectly fine with me. As long as I am in the same room with him, I am good.

In every relationship I have ever been in, I ALWAYS had trust issues. Lack of trust is the number one side effect experienced by those who have been sexually violated. Even after I got married, I started saying, "Why did you marry this guy if you can't trust him?" He and I would have conversations about my trust issues all the time. Honestly, I didn't think I deserved to be with a man that loved me completely. I desired it and had fantasies about having a man such as this, but now he was in my face and I didn't know what to do. I was about to destroy what I always wanted. **UNCONDITIONAL LOVE**. Love is a powerful four-letter word; to some, it may seem unreachable. Open your heart to the possibility. I knew I wanted true love, but my heart wasn't open. I still had walls up; literally surrounding me. I chose to let them down so that I could experience the love my husband had for me. It's good, too! Quite delicious. (smile) I began knocking down the walls, brick by brick. I had to be intentional in trusting him. Day by day, little by little I learned to let go and allow myself to be loved by my husband. No more will you allow fear, pain or hurt to rob you of the love you deserve. Love is there for the taking. You must believe it can happen for you as well. I'm so glad I did because my life has not been the same. I can't imagine it without my best friend and the love of my life.

My father literally robbed me of my childhood when he made the decision to molest me.

CHAPTER 6

It Was Not My Fault!

YOU KNOW WHAT? Hell no, it's not my fault! It's not my fault that my father molested me! I didn't do anything wrong...this is NOT my fault! The fact that my father sexually molested me? That was all of his selfish reasoning. It had nothing to do with me. It's NOT my fault! And NO, how can it be my fault when I was just a toddler? How can it be possible that I would entice a grown ass man? I mean my body was a "Baby Body"! That is absolutely disgusting to see a BABY as a sex object. This foolishness went on when I was a child so how the hell could this be my fault? How do I have power over an adult to make a decision?

He was stupid and reckless for even committing the violation. As I think about what happened to me as a child, some people would say, "Well, you have to take ownership of YOUR part in the violation." but I am not about to take ownership of a damn thing because I didn't do ANYTHING wrong! My father literally robbed me of my childhood when he made the decision to molest me. I grew up thinking I was already an adult. I grew up way too fast because my body experienced things that no child should experience before the age of consent. I always felt mature and unnaturally aware of my body. I knew exactly what I liked and didn't like when it came to sex. I should have had the privilege of enjoying cookies and milk, Barbie dolls, Cabbage Patch kids, paper dolls, and playhouses. Yes, I had all of those things, but that's ALL I should have been thinking about as a child. But instead, I was robbed. Instead of enjoying my childhood, I spent more time worrying if he was going to come into my room and bother me. I spent time worrying if I went to sleep next to my mom, would he try to fondle me? That was the worst feeling

EVER to have to always be on guard. No child should have to always wonder if anyone can be trusted. But even after all of that, I KNOW I did nothing wrong!

As I said, there is nothing I could have done to entice a grown ass man, especially the man who was not an uncle, cousin or next door neighbor. This was my father. The one who was supposed to protect me. The man who was supposed to make sure no one else ever took advantage of me but instead he made the choice to strip away my childhood. I can never get those years back.

As a therapist, my clients who are survivors of rape, molestation, incest and other horrific sexual encounters, the first thing most of them say is, "It's my fault." Then I ask, "What makes it your fault?" They began to say what they could have done differently like not going out late that night.. Yes, it's unfortunate this happened to me and others who were victimized, but NO ONE should have to take on the responsibility or the ownership of their perpetrator. No one should have to say, "If there was something I could have changed..." or "Why didn't I stop it?" or "Why did I wear that short dress or mini skirt?" Some women torture themselves by asking, "Why did I have to wear my hair like that or my makeup that way?" or "Why did I go over there?" NO! It was not YOUR fault either!

I refuse to allow you to take on the responsibility of your offender. The decision to violate you came solely from the decision of the perpetrator! You are not a victim; you are victorious. I empathize with those of you who may feel like you brought this on, but you do not have to own or accept what your perpetrator did. IT WAS NOT YOUR FAULT! I don't care if you were in the middle of a consensual sex act, when you say, "No" the answer is still, "No"! It's not your fault that the perpetrator made a poor choice to violate you. I *need* you to understand that this is not your fault! Don't continue to hold on to that responsibility. Give that ownership back to the offender. I don't care what kind of assault it was - rape, molestation, incest, or whatever type of offense it is; it is not your fault. Even if they said, "Had you not done *that* or said *this,* it would not have happened to you...", don't believe the lies anymore!

Don't listen to the people who do not understand the violation you've experienced. You didn't ask for ANY of this! You didn't ask for the deep hurt, sorrow, guilt, shame, anger, sadness, suicidal thoughts, homicidal thoughts or any pain...you did not ask for that! That was something that was placed upon you by a very selfish person. You were forced to encounter someone who didn't think of anyone but themselves and their self-pleasing gratification. Don't let the negative thoughts of, "would've-could've-should've" stay in your mind any longer. It is unfortunate that we were chosen for this violation. I say "chosen" because the perpetrator made a choice to choose you. I am so sorry this horrible violation has happened to you, but IT WAS NOT YOUR FAULT!

For years I was angry with my father for what he did to me, but I felt more compassion for him than anger.

You despise me! How dare you molest your own daughter, you are a nasty disgusting person. Parents are supposed to love not hurt their children. You were to protect me, not abuse me, and not destroy me. You only thought of your selfish desires and wants. NOT ME!!!!!!!!!!!!!! How could you? Who does that to their child, any child? I'll tell you who, a man that isn't a man. You are a monster, a snake, a filthy nasty creature. You don't have a heart. You can't! Anyone that has a heart would've known that this disgusting act would damage a child for life. You only thought about yourself. You've always thought about yourself. You beat my mom, and my siblings for trivial reasons (STUPID, idiotic reasons). What man tries to control his family with fear? A coward, that's what you are a coward. You sneaked around with other women, and doing God knows what else when you weren't at home. That's why that man shot you for messing around with his wife. I'm glad he shot you; actually I wish you were dead. You disrespected my mother for too many years. A woman that had your back was your partner in life and you mistreated her. You are a worthless piece of shit. I remember the stories my siblings would tell me about you. How you would beat them for not washing dishes, taking out the trash or just anything else you wanted to get mad about. I fanaticized about you dying. At the age of 6 or 7, I thought about ways of killing myself. I wanted to rid myself from your hateful ways. I wanted you to just drop off the face of the earth. I still do. I hate all the pain you have caused this family, all the tears my mother cried behind and over your stupid ass. All of my siblings having issues to this day because of you, either they don't know how to be a parent or they give their children everything. Still, this is because of you and how we were raised. I HATE YOU!!!!!! I hate that you never cared for anyone but yourself. Stop saying you love us. You don't know what love is or what it means. You are pathetic. I'm tired of thinking about you, carrying stress in my body, having somatic sxs all because of you. Today!!! I'm taking my power back. You are literally dead to me. I may continue to do things for you, if I want to. I will no longer feel obligated to protect you and/or do out of respect for you because you are my father. I will do things if I want to do them for you, then and only then. You are no longer a problem for or to me. I am burying you along with all this pain I have carried around for too many years. Goodbye, I'll see you when I see you.

Actual letter to my father when I was in therapy (2015)

CHAPTER 7

Pain to Power

ANGER. IT'S AN emotion often misunderstood. For years, I was angry with my father for what he did to me, but I felt more compassion for him than anger. I felt sorry for him. My gut tells me he experienced sexual abuse as a child so he, in turn, inflicted his pain on me. I don't believe what my dad did to me was malicious, I truly believe he was sick and completely out of control. Do you know who I was most angry with? **My mother.** I know some of you may say, "Lynn, how in the world could you be angry with your mother? She was a victim of abuse, too." The part that makes me angry is she could have protected me from a grown man, but she put her "love" for him over protecting me. It makes me angry she did not have enough self- respect not to allow my father not only violate me repeatedly, but she allowed him to dishonor her as his wife.

As I am writing this book, my mom is dealing with dementia. It makes me sad how she is not as jovial or aware of what is going on all the time. She is not the woman she used to be because she deals with depression, and even though her health is not the best, I was angry with her. I remember asking her if she remembered how he abused her. She claimed she did not remember. I just don't believe her. I believe she trained herself to forget the 55 years of pain she allowed in her dysfunctional relationship with my father. How does a human being forget abuse? How does a mother forget she prepared her child's body to be sexually abused by the man who was to protect her? I was angry with my mother because I felt she made it a habit to pretend none of this really happened. The pain of knowing the woman who gave birth to you could no longer remember the pain inflicted upon her baby girl is a sickening thought. I was angry.

I was also annoyed that no matter how much I explained my pain, it seemed as though it went in one ear and out of the other. Why was she doing this? Why did she refuse to remember the abuse? I think I could handle it better if she conveniently forgot the pain I endured but to forget your *own* abuse seems unreasonable...almost a joke.

My mother never told me I was lying about the abuse, but she just simply said, "I don't remember". Really, Mom? You don't remember? Even when my siblings would remind her of how my father used to beat on them and her, she simply denied it. So Mom, are you telling me all the pain we, as a family, have gone through was all a lie? Was this a fairytale? A nightmare that lasted over a half a century? My father was not only physically and sexually abusive but he was also emotionally abusive. Mom, you don't remember that? That pissed me off. I go between being angry with her and feeling compassion for her because dementia is NOT a fairytale. I get angry with myself at times because I'm like, "Lynn, lighten up! The woman is SICK. Give her a break!"

But the truth is, while she is sick, I long for her to take full ownership of her part in the dysfunction, abuse, and pain we endured at the hands of my father. I love my mother but I was MAD at her because she doesn't "remember". Or did she WILL herself to forget what happened? Did she train her brain to forget the pain? I understand her brain is not what it used to be but I am mad she doesn't remember! Perhaps there are some things she has forgotten but I did not believe she forgot everything.

One day, she apologized to me.

Even though my mother apologized to me, I still had residue from the past. Can you relate? Do you have residue from your past pain keeping you from colliding with your purpose? Just because you feel anger from time to time does not mean you have not forgiven. It simply means your body, mind, and spirit is processing the pain. Acknowledging your truth does not mean you haven't forgiven. It simply means you are human and may need to talk it through. Don't get me wrong; I love my parents, but just because you love someone does not mean you do not have the right to be angry with them. There is a major difference in feeling anger and *living* in anger. When you LIVE in anger, you look for reasons to humiliate and expose people. But it is perfectly okay to express your feelings in a healthy way causing you to move from pain to power!

Okay, let's talk about pain to power. As you know, I had so much hate for my father and the pain was deep. As the years have come and gone, I have forgiven the man that caused so much pain in my childhood that I carried to my adult years. Slowly, my heart began to mend and feel lighter. I was able to talk about him without the stabbing pain in my heart or in my body. As a matter of fact, my heart started to feel again. It was a stone for many years and now open to receive. I think about the song "Give Me a Clean Heart" by Fred Hammond. The lyrics are truly a testament on how I feel now.

My father passed away on January 1, 2019. New Year's Day. This day is usually symbolizing a new start in life. It was a day I got redemption, but not in a bad way. I had infinite closure. I lost my dad. For a long time, I pictured him to be a monster, an evil spirit. I had reduced him to be an inanimate object in my life. He was a "thing" to me and in my life. Over the years being in my healing place, he has become my father and a man. He is a person and no longer an object. I remember my father, my dad now. He had a sweet and sultry voice. He was a baker and a damn good one too. He was funny and made me laugh all the time; well, we made each other laugh. We shared jokes and we were both music connoisseurs. We shared a life outside of the abuse and violence. We loved each other and I had forgotten that because the pain wouldn't let me remember, but now the power is present and it has turned into purpose.

I *miss* my dad.

I have completely forgiven him. I also forgive myself for allowing me to miss out on life. I now stand strong and fearless and my purpose is to help others heal.

I spent so much time carrying secrets and being silent about my father sexually molesting me...

CHAPTER 8

Silent No More

EVEN THOUGH I am a licensed therapist, I only went to counseling three times in my life. One of those times was when I was a teenager, and I was forced to go. I was forced because I lied about being suicidal one day. The ambulance was called and they rushed me to the ER. It woke everyone in my family up, including me. I knew I was hurting at this time but didn't know how to say I was. The song that was playing in my hospital room was, *Hold On* by Wilson Philips. Being forced is never a good idea for those that want true healing. When you force someone to do something, they do it for various reasons. To shut you up, to avoid an argument, to save face, or fulfill a recommendation, but rarely to deal with the pain and heal.

The second time was when I was in college, and my professor encouraged me to go since I was studying to become a therapist. The last time I went to see a counselor was when I was still experiencing the residue from my past rearing its ugly head from time to time. I was still lashing out and becoming extremely angry when it didn't seem as if I was getting my way.

I went to counseling again before I got married. I felt like I needed to begin healing before I tore my relationship completely apart and I didn't want to bring it into my marriage. By this time, I had already found my voice, but I knew I had to get this toxic residue out of me once and for all. As I have shared with you before, give the pain back to the perpetrator. In my case, I had to give the pain back to my father. I had finally found my voice, but I still had some pain and hurt that I held on to. Counseling helped me to give that pain back my father. I never wished that he experienced the pain he inflicted on me, but I just needed him to know that I am not responsible for the pain he caused me. I was no longer going to allow him to keep me silent through manipulation and intimidation...I became

SILENT NO MORE! After speaking my truth, I felt bold and courageous, like the warrior I was destined to be.

When I began to speak my truth, it literally came up and out of me like vomit. My very soul was being purged just by speaking my truth with boldness and no longer allowing shame to keep me muzzled. The more I purged, the better I felt. Have you ever been getting ready to vomit and you feel it bubbling up? Then, you try to find the nearest bathroom because you know this thing is about to come out! That nasty taste begins to fill your mouth and then... YUCK it's everywhere. When you first tell your truth, that's how it may feel, but once you get it out of you, you start to feel better. It feels terrible when it first comes out but once it's out, you don't have to experience that pain ever again. That's how I felt when I first told my story--relieved.

What do you do when you want to use your voice to speak up about a situation, and someone tries to shut you down? What about the voice in your head that says, "Shut up!" when you muster up the courage to finally tell your story? How do you handle the moment when you are in a group setting, and other people are so bravely telling their stories and just before you are about to tell yours the facilitator says, "That's it for tonight," and everyone leaves the room. You may be thinking to yourself, "Who's going to listen to me? Does anyone care about my story? Maybe I should just keep it to myself." Many of your perpetrators have placed a muzzle or a metal plate with chains over your mouth and have forbidden you to say anything about what they put you through.

I spent so much time carrying secrets and being silent about my father sexually molesting me that I forgot the sound of my own voice. Many of us were taught, "What goes on in this house, stays in this house" which is the biggest lie on the planet! When it feels like you don't have a voice, it seems like you can disappear right into the ground. So many times I felt invisible, inferior and inadequate. On the inside, I was SCREAMING at the top of my lungs, but my mouth was completely shut, and I was not making a sound. I know what it's like to feel like a hand has been permanently placed over your mouth and all you wanted to do was pry it off, but it just remains there. Allow me to coach you into getting your voice back.

Quite frankly, some of you have probably never had a voice, but that stops right now! Allow me to give you the key to unlock your voice. Your story can help free so many people who are dealing with what you are currently going through or what you have overcome. Don't allow anyone to put a muzzle on you and keep you in bondage ANYMORE! You no longer have to be held captive to the pain of your past. What you have to say is valid even if it is painful to repeat. Even if you feel insecure or your self-esteem is at an all-time low, you don't have to be silent anymore.

Even when a child first learns to speak, they may mumble or use baby words like, "mama" or "da da," but at least they are using their voice. In the wake of the #MeToo movement, even if you can start with that, it's time for you to be silent no more. It does not take a lot of words to speak your truth. Just like that baby who says their first words, I give you permission to just make a sound. Then, make another sound. And keep going until you have spoken your truth. Speak YOUR truth, not the lies that will make others feel comfortable. Even if you have to write it down, you don't have to be silent anymore!

Now some of you may be saying, "What's the benefit of unleashing my voice?" The first benefit is you get to say what YOU want to say and no longer be afraid of the opinions of others. Your need for change is not for their benefit but YOUR benefit. When you use your voice, you have the opportunity to address what your perpetrator has done and not allow them to have any power over you through silence. When you realize you have a voice, you have the opportunity to celebrate your wins and successes in life. If you do not feel successful, that's okay. You have the chance to rewrite the narrative of your life to experience the life of your dreams. You no longer have to dummy down or feel minimized because of the poor choice of your perpetrator. Your voice not only matters, it must be heard and respected.

Your complete healing will come through sharing your story. There are steps to take in your healing process so allow yourself time, patience, understanding. Forgive those who have hurt you and most importantly, FORGIVE YOURSELF. Don't let your voice be silenced due to past mistakes. I am not saying you have to take the stage or write a book like me, but please tell someone you trust your story. You don't even have to know them very well, just tell someone and allow your heart to vent. Allow your soul to be emptied from the pain. Give yourself permission to speak your truth and fight for your healing by using the healing waters of your voice as the prescription for your pain. Purge your spirit of the dark cloud of secrets and violations that may haunt you on a daily basis.

When you hold on to hurt, you become toxic with the propensity to contaminate others. Please don't allow the cancer of silence to make or keep you sick because you refuse to speak up about your truth. Speak to a therapist, a friend or a spiritual leader but just get that poison out of your system so that you may begin the healing process. I give you permission to be SILENT NO MORE!

Give yourself some compassion and don't keep this pain bottled up anymore. You owe yourself the right to speak your truth no matter who won't like it. Start speaking life and kindness to your spirit instead of the negativity that life presents to you. When life starts going in a way we don't want it to go, we tend to speak negatively about the situation; but, be kind to yourself even during the challenging times. Don't listen to the cowards who say you are stupid, worthless or helpless. Don't listen to the naysayers who say you don't matter because you *do* matter! I reverse those negative words spoken over your life! You are NOT stupid. You are NOT worthless. You are NOT helpless you are a survivor who has a voice with its own unique identity. I used to think I didn't matter either. I used to think my voice had a permanent lock on it. In the back of my mind, I knew it was a lie, but somehow, I tried to keep the lie going in my head. I finally realized that whatever a person thinks, that's what they are. So, I need you to believe nothing but good, lovely, honorable and excellent things about yourself. I had to train myself to speak beautiful, positive, pleasant and excellent affirmations over my body to replace the misery that had been deposited into my soul when I was a baby. I had to detox and get that junk out of me. Just like when you eat a lot of junk food, at some point, you have to detox your body, or you will become sick. Yes, the junk food may taste good temporarily, but at some point, it will backfire on you and cause discomfort. Those processed foods were not made for us to consume and remain healthy. So it is with negative words that are spoken over us, or that we speak over ourselves during a moment of weakness. When you have been a victim of sexual abuse, you may think you deserve the negative words and that it's "good" that you are hearing those words, but that is a lie!

These are some affirmations that have helped me. I hope they are beneficial for you as well.

- *Recovery is absolutely possible and achievable for me.*
- *I will practice being disloyal to dysfunction and loyal to functionality.*
- *I give myself permission to connect to loving, affirmative, strong, sensitive, accepting men and women in my community.*
- *I release and forgive myself for any responsibility I have accepted in the past for my abuse.*
- *The abuser(s) from the past chose to hurt me.*
- *I will stop repeating the lie that it just happened to me.*
- *Offering myself daily compassion is necessary for my healing and growth.*
- *I commit to connecting to the (girl) inside me today so we can play, laugh, and experience joy together, even if it's just for a minute or two.*
- *I believe deep inside me I possess the ability to face the truth of my abuse and to learn to use new tools for healing.*
- *I have the right and the ability to speak the truth of my abuse and deserve to be heard, understood, believed, and supported.*
- *Feeling is healing. As I heal, I develop the ability to experience multiple emotions to enhance my mental health and interpersonal relationships.*

Please feel free to create affirmations that speak to you.

The second benefit of unleashing your voice is you will begin to believe in yourself and your abilities. Whoever you deem as your Higher Power, I suggest you become more acquainted with a force greater than yourself. My Higher Power is God, the Creator of Heaven and Earth. If it weren't for Him, I would have no voice. My relationship with my Lord and Savior, Jesus Christ, is the one that strengthened me when I felt like taking my own life. I knew that even though I felt abandoned by my family many times throughout my life; I knew that God would never let me down. Some people say, "I don't like religion," but that is not what I said. What I *am* saying is you must have a spiritual connection greater than yourself to truly unleash your voice and maintain your strength.

The third benefit of unleashing your voice is the need to engage in self-care. Many survivors of sexual abuse have the propensity to neglect themselves due to feelings of worthlessness. You cannot help your significant other, children, or even be successful in your career if you do not engage in self-care. From great hygiene to getting the proper nutrition on a daily basis, self-care is not a suggestion but a necessity. Go on and take that bubble bath or invest in a hot stone massage. Do any and everything you need to do to make you feel good about yourself. Many women love a good manicure, pedicure and a much-needed trip to the hair salon. Men have the option to engage in a good old fashion fishing trip with the guys or a fun weekend in Vegas. Whatever it takes for you to recharge and take care of your mind, body, and spirit, I give you permission to do just that. Some of you may be saying, "Well, I do those things already and still feel like crap!" If we are honest, some of us do those things to impress other people but do whatever it takes to take care of yourself! It's so much easier to tell your story when you feel good about yourself. And it will be easier to maintain your healing when you make self-care your top priority. Have you ever given YOURSELF a bear hug? Ok, take a moment right now and squeeze yourself as tight as you can. That's called loving on yourself. The more you love on yourself, the more you will be SILENT NO MORE!

You don't always have to spend money to love on yourself because some things are free. Take a moment and just sit with your thoughts. Have you ever thought about who YOU really are? Not what people say you are but who do YOU say you are? Sit in that and embrace it. You are amazing and beautifully made by the Creator. Take a moment and celebrate your wins from just today. Don't try to rehearse the last five years of what you did right, how about you just celebrate today?

Changing your mindset is going to be critical in your healing process. I used to categorize myself as a victim until I decided to remove that label and become a survivor. And just like me, YOU ARE NO LONGER A VICTIM! Did I go through trauma, hurt and pain? Yes! But I am not a victim; I am a survivor. Did I ever feel helpless or worthless? Absolutely! But I am not a victim; I am a warrior. When I realized I could take back my voice and I could take back my power, I became a **Surviving Warrior!** I literally kicked my trauma in the BUTT the moment I decided that I would not allow the weapon of silence to keep me in fear of telling my story. I made a conscious decision not to allow the molestation from my father to have power over me.

Ask God to show you who you can trust with your story. Whether it is a therapist, a pastor, a family member or friend, it's time to tell your story. Find a tribe who can help you voice your pain in a way you won't feel judged. I am here to help you. You are not alone. You are welcomed to join my tribe, **"The Surviving Warriors"** which is a safe community for survivors of sexual abuse. The Surviving Warriors share their stories, swap advice and support one another as we move from pain to purpose. Email me at lynn@survivingwarriors.org or visit www.survivingwarriors.org and allow me to show you how to find and unleash your voice. I don't care if I have to help you *sing* it out, just tell your story! Do whatever you have to do to get comfortable with your *own* voice. The main thing I need you to realize is, you are not defined by what happened to you. Despite the fact that this was an ugly experience, you are beautiful! The lie you were told is you didn't matter, the truth is that you are EVERYTHING! You do exist and others see you, in all your beauty. I LOVE YOU! Speak your truth, tell your story; say something. Be bold, powerful, confident and courageous. You don't have to be silent anymore. Being a victim of sexual abuse is NO LONGER AN OPTION!

About The Author

Lynn Meyer is a world-class Licensed Professional Counselor specializing in judgment-free therapy since 2003. Her unique therapeutic system will teach you valuable tools on how to make your life better, even if it is not what you want to hear. Lynn will help you develop a plan for change based on your very own personal feelings and priorities. Whether you are dealing with Depression, abuse (sexual, physical, & emotional), ineffective communication, mood disorders, or trauma, Lynn is committed to helping you break free.

www.ingramcontent.com/pod-product-compliance
Lightning Source LLC
LaVergne TN
LVHW051815080426
835513LV00017B/1959